Strive

by

Jennifer Brown

RoseDog Books
PITTSBURGH, PENNSYLVANIA 15238

RoseDog Books
585 Alpha Drive
Suite 103
Pittsburgh, PA 15238
Visit our website at *www.rosedogbookstore.com*

ISBN: 979-8-88729-285-4
eISBN: 979-8-88729-785-9

Contents

Introduction

The human mind has respect for any evil vainglory that happens overnight. In fact, it studies it. However, the human mind does not respect nor remember any good thing from God that is given instantly upon request. In fact, the quick, miraculous deeds of the Lord God Almighty are quickly forgotten. Take the children whom Moses led in the desert for 40 years. Thus, the discipline of our "Abba" (father) is taught slowly so that the human being may shift change in stages.

The human mind can only recall understanding through a time framed by God. Patience is a fruit of the Spirit of God from which we gain understanding and a clear mind of remembrance of who we are. The human was created weak to the flesh yet fearfully made by the Spirit through test, problems, and trials. You were created in the presence of the enemy by God Himself and the 24. The enemy does not want you to remember who you are.

Every quick fix is from the enemy who gives you a taste of anything harmful to the memory that relieves stress and temporarily distracts you from reality. It is his duty to give you a quick fix of forgetfulness. And why does your Father not allow the quick fix to last? Because He does not want you to forget who you are. Saints! You were made saints through striving past problems, trial, and tribulation. "Or do you think that you will enter the Garden while there has not yet befallen you the like of what befell those who have passed away before you. Distress and affliction befell them…" {2:14}.

> *Count it all joy my brothers, when you meet trials of various kinds, for you know that the testing of your faith produces steadfastness. And let steadfastness have its full effect that you may be perfect and complete lacking in nothing.*
>
> *– James 1:2-4*

Therefore, walk in the spirit and not the flesh, for the spirit remembers to strive while the flesh forgets. Once I tell you who you are, truly, I say you shall gain the power God gave His saints. Forget not your Maker and control the flesh, for flesh is just lust inside the body. Power to gain mind control over your body shall come after your eyes become open to knowing "self." I give thanks to God and praise Him in total truth, for I have been graced with the command to open the eyes of the blind. Doing so through this knowledge that only God can provide will place back the crown that was removed from your head.

If you seek for a quick fix, it is because your spirit is anti-errored. It is in an era of error. A timing of bad condition and a condition of bad timing. It is, indeed, evil for the spirit to search for things considered a "quick fix," for all things that are fixed quickly despises (hates) the Spirit of Truth. All things invented by the enemy of God is able to "quickly fix," yet by God's power, is unable to last simply because it was easily and quickly fixed.

The human mind will surely search desperately and wholeheartedly for a quick problem dissolver again and over again until they have wasted a greater amount of time than it would have taken for the human mind to shift change in phases. It is a programmed survival mechanism. Although your Abba (Father) is able to say to all things "Be" and it becomes, God does not say "Be" unto the darkness in the heart of man, for the human being will not respect nor remember Abba-Kaddabrah!

Count the number of tribes aloud and be still. This is a tool used to exercise patience. Begin to count from one to 12 without moving a single muscle below the mouth. Be very still. Repeat the count next in your mind, and this time, without moving a single bone below your nose. If you notice any movement, start over again until you perfect this doing. This means war. The act signifies that, originally, you were forgetful, and now, you again remember who you were created to be.

1

The Making

You were created of dust and a liquid sperm drop (a small life germ). With this clay, you were molded and fashioned. Every exquisite feature and construction of your fingerprint was to be feared and examined by the 24 scientists that encamp around the throne of Allah (which means all the names of God). These 24 elders marveled over you and even began to count the hairs on your head. Your posture was made upright. A crown with "St" was placed on your head, for you were made saints! A crown symbolizing life.

God looked through your eyes, seeing where you would go and who you would become. At that moment, your destiny and future were written in a book by the scientists who calculate up to 5,000 years at a lifetime. Our Maker, who stretched out the heavens and laid the foundations of the Earth, gave you many gifts when you were created by them. Yes, they all took turns perfecting you the way they liked in their imagination; from your forehead to your pinky toe. "And certainly you have come to Us one by one as We created you at first..." {6:94}.

...Then God said, "Let <u>us</u> make man in <u>our</u> image, after <u>our</u> likeness..." They then gifted you power you still do not know you have. God then placed specific authority upon you. Remember this.

– Genesis 1:26

2

Jealousy Borne in Heaven

When God saw the finished work of you, He said to the multitude of angels: "Bow down before man."

The angels bowed down to you and accepted your crown of authority, except for Satan, whose spirit is called "devil." He did not bow down. He stood as God was standing; challenging God's actions. To God's unsurprised surprise, He witnessed the birth of an error in His courtyard.

God asked, "What is it that hindered you from bowing down?"

And he said, "I am better than this creation, for You made me out of fire and him out of dust."

God said, "Get down from it [that it is the high horse that Satan sat upon in the loft of his proud spirit of error]; it is not for you to act arrogantly in it [Satan's dome]. You shall be cast out, you despot!"

Satan answered, "Give me respite."

The Lord said, "You are among those who have respite."

The enemy, in his anger, began to convince a number of the angels, giving them ample reason to oppose God, for he was present to witness the make of you; where you would go and who you would become. He said, "I will go before them and come from behind them and from their right side and their left and cause them to deviate from Your straight path where they were made to go, and You won't find most of them appreciative."

And God responded, "Whosoever follows you, I will fill up hell with you all!"

And 665 Angels sided with Lucifer, giving themselves the title "Kings of Persia."

3

Straight Path

Fair game! Life on Earth is nothing but forgetfulness and distraction. "But ye are Saints and not barbarians for you were built to last." Life is like a strong wind that comes to devour houses built by men; afterwards, only the houses built by God stood standing. Or it's like an earthquake that violently shook the earth to cast down what was weak to distinguish what is strong. Only the strong survive and enter into the Garden, which beneath it, rivers flow.

You were put here to strive, to endure, to <u>remember</u> and not <u>forget who you are.</u> To partake of the last men standing.

*Blessed is the man that endureth temptation; for when he is tried (passed the test), he shall receive the *<u>crown of life</u>*, which the Lord has promised…*

— James 1:12

*But be ye doers of the word and not hearers only, deceiving your own selves. For if any be a hearer of the word, and not a doer, he is like a man beholding <u>his natural face in a glass</u> (mirror) (finding self): for he beholdeth (sees) *himself* and goes away, and straightway (quickly) forgets what manner of man he was (how - who - what he was made to be) But he who looks into the <u>perfect law</u> (straight path), law of*

Amen? Selah.

Satan promised to waylay us all from following the straight path;
all who were weak, surrendering to the devil (evil inside "self"), giving
in to the passions of the flesh; therefore, falling victim to sin. Yet only
by God's power the weak who strive are made strong. God, after making you, reversed your time. He recapitulated your years and placed
you into the man who put you in your mother's stomach, and in the
straight path of perfect peace, which God calls Islam. "No longer shall
they suffer, nor shall they grieve." In the path of righteousness, no
weapon formed against you will prosper. Nothing at all shall harm you.
No one shall even touch the anointed ones nor the prophets in the
straight path.

But the human being has deviated to other dark paths of sorrow
and unrighteousness, as the enemy promised. It is a fixed path. You
yourself choose to walk in it. The straight path of Perfect Law is also
available for you to walk in. Choose to walk in it, for it is a fixed path
where destruction and harm is surely made to swerve around you. On
all other paths lay all the things that keep you blind and bound to the
slavery of whatever is "god" to you. These paths are fixed to the respite
of the (Devil) evil inside yourself.

That God may make what casts at them become a trial for those in whose hearts is a brick wall and a disease {22:53}. If this guide were to condemn you, I would be teaching touching the subject of the "Law of <u>Sins Sizes,</u>" but the command to lead you to your identity is to be obeyed. Do not fear nor reject the guide of God by choosing to hold fast to the sin you so admire. Instead, choose life so that you and your children may live! (See Deuteronomy 30:11-19).

<u>By the grace of God, the Beneficent, the Merciful,</u>
<u>He provides for you a backroad…</u>
<u>A road in which He has commanded His angels to construct at the very end of each path of destruction.</u>
<u>You who finds the backroad, to you, opportunity is given; for the backroad leads you to return unto the Straight Path. Glory, honor, power, and praise be to the Lord God who has caused your eye to follow into this backroad towards the straight path. You are now in the Valley of Decision {Joel 3:14}. Take a good look at this map's fixed direction.</u>

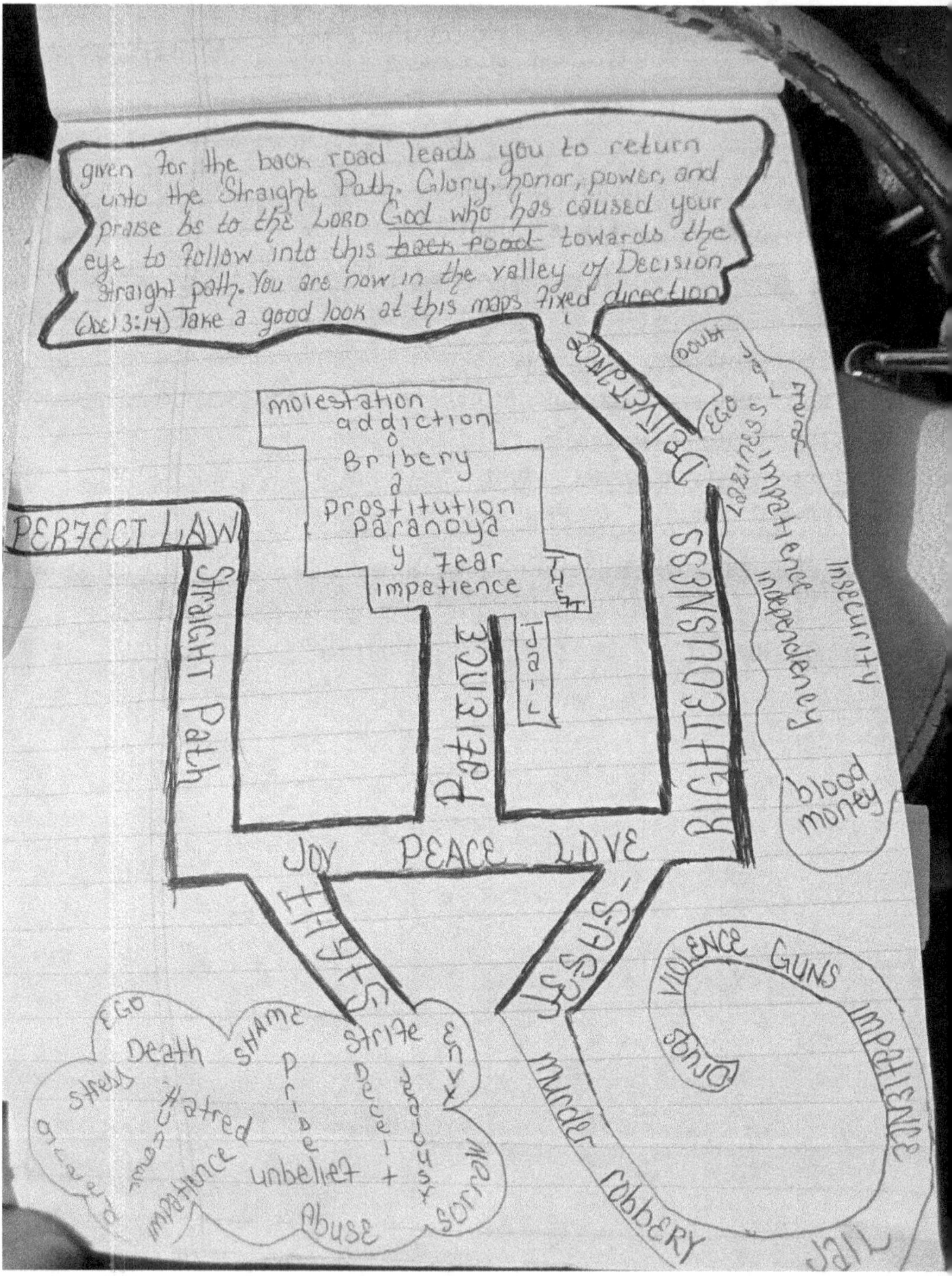

given for the back road leads you to return unto the Straight Path. Glory, honor, power, and praise be to the Lord God who has caused your eye to follow into this ~~back road~~ towards the Straight path. You are now in the valley of Decision (Joel 3:14) Take a good look at this maps fixed direction

PERFECT LAW

Straight Path

molestation
addiction
Bribery
prostitution
paranoya
fear
impatience

PATIENCE

Theft
Jail

JOY   PEACE   LOVE

RIGHTEOUSNESS

DELIVERANCE

doubt
EGO
fear
laziness
impatience
independency
insecurity
blood money

JESUS-IS-

FAITH

EGO
stress
Death   SHAME   strife
pride
Hatred   deceit
impatience   unbelief   towardness   sorrow
Abuse

murder   robbery

DRUGS   VIOLENCE   GUNS
IMPATIENCE
JAIL

4

God Speed

The Creator of the wind, seas, and snow is your Maker. He hears every thought and sees every hidden thing you do. He is the greatest Seer and Knower. "And certainly We create man, and We know what his mind suggests unto him—and We are nearer to him than his life vein" {50:16}.

Your Maker embedded the genes in your DNA, and before placing you in your mother's womb, He knew you and ordained you.

> *Before I formed thee in the belly I knew thee, and before you came forth out of the womb I sanctified thee, and I ordained thee a...*
>
> *– Jeremiah 1:5*

God said, "Today, I have perfected it for you, I choose Islam as your religion. It is the straight path in which ye are to walk and follow." Be not waylaid from the path of peace, for destruction and impatience is surely set firm in all other paths.

The day of devastation cannot be delayed nor forwarded by one hour. The day of judgment is surely appointed to meet every creature. It is a day you can trust to approach, for it is promised to you. There is a place of torment where there is fire and brimstone to scorch the flesh off the face of every man therein. And they shall thirst, but flames shall their souls be given to drink.

In those days, the burning soul would complain and blame the ones who further caused them to wallow in the path of destruction while the faithful warners and you, who believe and did not reject God's teaching in this guide, relax and recline on couches in the peaceful Garden, which, beneath it, flows rivers of milk and streams of honey. Youth shall never cease to serve you, and every tree will be in your reach. Total satisfaction forever is the reward, and the very atmosphere is your high, for you will experience a long, everlasting "fix" where certain emotions no longer exist within you. Your ears shall finally tickle to the definition of heavenly music. A sound unheard of by the cleanliness of the saints and sopranoed by the best of birds. Your heart will forget to beat at first glance of the Kingdom, for the mind will fail to comprehend an explanation in communication to your sight: Behold, the glory of the Lord, your God, the Great I Am That I Am.

Those who passed up the opportunity, to them, will be the melting pot. When the skin has been swallowed up by the grill of the wrath of God, He replaces the flesh so that those who did not obey the Lord and Messenger repeatedly feel the boil and fry of fresh flesh. It is agony. This is the reality of the results of the choices we make today in this life. Do not forget your Maker nor who you are.

5

Identity Theft

Do you not know that you are a chosen generation? A royal priesthood? Do you not know who you are? I am come to tell you who you are. I command, demand, declare, and decree sight to the eye that has strived unto this point. And to the ear; I speak into it. I prophesy unto your hearing—hearing has multiplied and comes now hearing to your ear. The ears now completely understand what the eyes read. Behold, the scales have fallen, and inclination has taken its toll. The eye can now speak, and the ear now see by the Word of God saying, "My Lord, lead me in through an entry of Truth and lead me out through an exit of Truth and grant me from You a supporting power. Truth has come and falsehood has withered away, for falsehood is bound to wither away."

Fear not! You were created with authority and powers you know not you have. You remember vaguely of these God-given attributes. When you were a child, you knew you had certain kinds of supernatural Powers because "the powers that 'Be' are ordained of God." You even dreamed of the hosts of heaven (clouds, winds, trees, seas, and stars) entertaining you. Need I remind you that all the creation of God's chosen had these dreams? And now look! You had forgotten how special gods you were made to be since childhood.

The devil (evil in you) had caused you to forget who you are. Evil has robbed you of the memory of your name, your land, your title, your history, your language, your lineage (bloodline), your authority, and your mind power! In this guide is an attempt made to lead you that you may return to God through sight and hearing by the Spirit of God! Perhaps you had replaced the memory of who you were created to be with low "self" esteem of who you currently are and all the darkness you have been entangled in while walking beyond the fixed path of destruction.

Here is reconstruction and instruction. It is time. And in time is order built to rebuild buildings. God said, "Any place where my gods [the chosen] are caused to hear my voice shall a <u>breach repairer</u> [a back road] be wherein which they walk toward my straight path where there is law [fixed]." This is the grace of your Father, God, for He has caused you to redirect in a position to incline your ear. Will you hear? For He guides whomever He wills and leaves astray whomever He wills. The Lord God is righteous and just in His judgment.

And it is not of God that He should lead you astray after He has guided you so whomsoever He intends to guide; He expands their heart for Islam and whomsoever He intends to leave astray, He allows them to continue with pride and ignorance. Thus does Allah lay unrighteousness on those in whose hearts are a defect and infection. As to you who believe, He that has begun a great work in you is faithful to perform it so far so that He makes clear to you what you should guard against.

For this purpose was your ears made in a threefold connection to your eyes and processed to the command of your brain. Even cheese when it is <u>processed</u> becomes <u>imitation</u>. "But if <u>they will not</u> return unto me <u>I will not</u> force them." The human being is so unbelieving and ungrateful. It is the dark things which they hold dear to their hearts that causes it. They cherish their sin more than God. They do not truly believe He sees and do not truly believe He cares. Lies! I say it is a lie. They would much rather inquire about the former ways of the messenger to find a fault to lean upon it as a crutch in order to reject the message, justifying the wretched evil in the core of their soul.

Do they not know that the warners were the filthiest of the appointed of God, sent that they, like Paul, may relate to all kinds of flesh? Do they not know that God is not mocked and if a warner spoke lies about the Lord your God, He would surely know it! Be not led astray, but return; for it is to God you shall surely return on that promised day. "We have ordained death among you and We are not to be overcome, that We may change your state and make you grow into what you know not" {56:60- 61}. You are a powerful creation and mighty in power. You are fearful in authority and wonderful in declaration. <u>You are gods</u>.

6

Who Are You?

I have said, "Ye are gods; and all of you are children of the most High."
— Psalms 82:6

Jesus answered them and said, "Is it not written in your law, I said, 'Ye are god's'?"
— John 10:34

Surely you will remember yourself. The Holy Bible in Hebrew/Aramaic is truly the Word of God, the Gracious, the Merciful. However, upon translation, His Word has been revised and distorted! This was done to keep you from knowing who you are. There are now many contradictions—additions—and omissions.

How dare they rob you! To keep you in the low condition you are in for selfish gain of money and earthly power. Robbed you have been of the memory of your crown. Robbed you have been of the life. Only the Holy Spirit of God can lead you and the lost found reader to detect and connect the dots in verses of distortion and undistortion.

But who among the humans find time in the spirit of error to strive and figure out why they are confused or uncertain? Hence, they remain lost and ignorant in their impatience, so time cannot find them. These are they who purchase error for guidance, so their bargain brings no profit, nor are they guided but misled by distortion, so they lean on their own understanding and the understanding of those before them. The truth I share comes from God Himself who is also the same author of the Quran. This is also this same kind of parlance it gives that I gift to you yet unique in its time, for the Spirit of God moves me in 2021.

So, who are you? What is your name?

And ye shall leave <u>your name</u> for a curse unto <u>my chosen</u>: for the Lord God shall slay thee, and <u>call his servants by another name</u>:
– Isaiah 65:15

And so, who are you? And what is your name? That is not your name! It is time to take back your name. <u>Your last name does not belong to you</u>! You are Hebrew; children of Israel. You are Father Abram's off-spring. God changed his name to Abba Raham. Abba-Raham. From this point forward, every "Ab" name you run across in scripture is a father of an entire generation.

It is recorded in history and the Book (Bible) until this day that we, the chosen generation, the peculiar stiff-necked people of God, are the offspring of our forefathers Abraham, Ishmael, Isaac, and Jacob, whose name was changed to Israel (Genesis 32:28). It is we whose great-grand-parents were in slavery 400 years. No other people has been afflicted for this exact amount of years except for the black race.

Then the Lord said unto Abram, "Know for certain that your off-spring will be <u>sojourners in a land that is not theirs</u> and will be slaves there, and they will be afflicted 400 years."
– Genesis 15:13

Yes, you were of a Hebrew slave for Abraham was.

You are a Hebrew-Israelite.

Do you not know that if Loretta was sold to the Cunninghams, she became Loretta Cunningham; and if they shipped her to the Pittmans, she then became Loretta Pittman? And to the Shoemakers, Tamika became Tamika Shoemaker; and to the Lynches, you were David Lynch. Again:

You [our forefathers slave owner] shall leave your name [last name] to my chosen [you] as a curse [title signifying bondage]...but His servants He will call by another name.

– Isaiah 65:15

As of today, you are your first name. What you are is your ethnicity, which takes its place as a middle name. And your last name is the first name of your human father or mother, if you know not your father. For example, I am *Jennifer, the Hebrew-Israelite, daughter of Michael*. Just as Jesus, the Christ, Son of Mary.

Go ahead, write down your name for the first time, and witness the beauty of it, for <u>you are the only one on Earth with that name</u>. Until God changes your name, this is your true identity. Say your name and think about it. This is even how the Book identifies an individual's significance. Your current last name is a handcuff within itself. Though you carry a last name handed down from your forefathers' slave master, it is important that you know who you are while those in authority over you in certain exiles make sure your face matches the last name on your ID.

Though it may be standard practice for them to address those of you by the chain attached to your first name, you may say, "Call me by my first name," which should place fear in the heart of anyone who rules over those who rule over you. As long as you know who you are, you can look up and address your prayers to whom it may concern. God's children are called by their priesthood (identity) and chosen by their lineage (bloodline).

But you are a <u>chosen race</u>, a <u>royal priesthood</u>, a <u>holy nation</u>, a <u>people for his own possession</u> [God of Truth].

– 1 Peter 2:9

For thou art an holy people unto the Lord your God: The Lord your God has chosen you to be a <u>special people</u> unto himself, <u>above all people</u> that are upon the face of the earth.

– Deuteronomy 7:6

Every promise of the Lord God Almighty belongs to you: the Ab- original offspring. The children of Israel, tents of Judah, Zion, the peculiar stiff-necked people, Jerusalem; these are titles that replace your entity in the Book.

7

Mind Control

Now that you know who you are, you can now learn to practice the Power of Authority. This is mind control. Those who are controlled by the devil (evil within "self") allow Satan to rule over their mind. Let <u>not</u> the body tell the mind what to do because the Kingdom of God (Heaven) begins also in the mind. Aye! King-Dome. You are King in the dome over your body. You are the Head and not the tail, Ruler of the temple (mind), yes, the Holy temple above the church (body).

Therefore, you can live in heaven while on Earth. "Thy kingdom come, thy will be done on <u>earth as it is in heaven</u>." When you have control over your mind, you, then, by all means have control over the body. If you control the body, then the former (old) wicked ways become <u>completely forgotten</u>. There is nothing dark in the Kingdom of Heaven nor in a mind of light. Your reality becomes new and likewise different by mind control.

For behold, I create new heavens and a new earth, and <u>former things</u> *<u>shall not be remembered nor come into mind.</u>*

– Isaiah 65:17

Therefore, we fast to practice self-discipline. We do not let our body tell us when to satisfy it. We tell our body when it should be satisfied.

Let not your body tell you where it wants to go but let your mind tell your body to follow you instead. Practice now if you will. Use the restroom when you do not have to, and your body will utilize it at that moment. Do it often.

Reject not the guidance of God. "When ye are angry, sin not." When the blood boils and adrenaline is birthed, your body tells you to retaliate. I say to you: Do not so! Go and make the body to kneel before the Lord God and file the complaint report to Allah, your Maker.

"Vengeance is mine, I will repay": <u>Getting even does not belong to you</u>. No, it does not.

Refrain from it, and do not rob God of the chance to repay, for there is more than just pain and loss that accompanies His recompense. His vengeance comes with meaning; sorrow, pain, regret, growth, recognition, conviction, brainstorming, and a deep need for forgiveness by God and you.

8

Control the Law of the Universe

There is a power you did not believe in. It is a mighty God-given power of life and death. He gave it unto you because even He has it. Be cautious with it. When Allah created the universe, He commanded it to shape your fate based off what it hears you declaring and to offer to you what you act out as if you have. You cannot confuse the universe. It is only doing its job.

> *For we stumble in many ways, and if anyone does not stumble in what he says, he is a perfect man and able also to bridle [control] his whole body.*
>
> *– James 3:2*

Do you not know the severity of the power of your tongue? The Law God gave unto the universe is established by any language of the tongue and language of the body, which shapes life's entire direction. The tongue is a restless animal that cannot be tamed. If you stick it out of your mouth, it will not cease movement until you advance on how to control it also.

> *...and the tongue is a fire, a world of iniquity; so is the tongue among our members [body parts], that it <u>defiles the whole body</u>, and sets on*

fire the <u>entire course of life</u>, and is set on fire of hell.

– James 3:6

God said to the universe, "<u>So</u> a man thinketh <u>so</u> is he; Let the redeemed of the Lord <u>say so</u>." Think about this Law He distributed and to your control. It is, indeed, a Law of attraction. So do not say, "I am a winner," and walk about daily as though you think you are defeated, for the universe is only obeying its command to bring you defeat. "Speak things into existence, calling things that are not as though they were." You receive from the universe what you think you already have that which you hope for.

> *Now faith is the <u>assurance</u> [substance] of things hoped for, the conviction [evidence] of things not seen. For by it the people of old <u>received</u> their commendation. Through faith we understand that the universe was created by the word [say so] of God, so that <u>things which are seen were not made of things that are visible</u>.*

– Hebrews 11:1-3

> *For those who say such things thus make it clear that they are seeking a homeland [something hoped for]. If they had been thinking of that land [destination] from which they had gone out [came from] <u>they would have had</u> the opportunity to return.*

– Hebrews 11:14-15

This is a supernatural power that works if you walk about daily as if you believe the very thing you have spoken out into the air.

> *...and the world listens to them.*

– 1 John 4:5

It was commanded to hear you and to fetch you what you think is in your reach. It feeds off fear, for it has "the fear of the Lord." However, "God did not give you a spirit of fear and worry [paranoia] but a spirit of power, love, and a sound mind." Fear and worry come from the same path of destruction from which impatience also came.

Confuse not this kind of fear with the godly "Fear of the Lord," for fear of the Lord simply means "afraid of doing the wrong thing." Again, fear of the Lord means "afraid of doing the wrong thing."

"Oh universe cease not to spin and heed not unto the request of the spirit of error." The universe was taught how to differentiate between spirits. God said to it: "Identify it by its fruits; know them by their marks and recognize them by their tone of speech."

The spirit of error has not patience, which is a fruit of the Spirit of God. If you say you are happy yet act sad, you will get more sorrow from the universe, for you failed to confuse it. Our tongue is a sword that our minds sharpen. Let not your sword be dull. Birth a thing into existence and unbelief shall make it stillborn. The spirit of error is an <u>amiss</u> spirit of impatience.

> *You desire and do not have, so you murder. You covet and cannot obtain [get] so you fight and quarrel [argue]. You do not have because *you* do not ask [the Spirit of Truth is not making the request] you ask and do not receive, because you ask <u>amiss</u> [with spirit of error].*
>
> *– James 4:2-3*

9

Access to Power

You have access to certain gates of the Kingdom of Heaven while on Earth. You can be granted the ability to think, calculate, and function in different sections of the brain. I call it P.B.L. No, not "punishable by life," aha, aha. It is the "Power to Bind and Loose"!

*I will give you the <u>keys</u> [access] <u>to the kingdom</u> of heaven, and *<u>wha-tever</u>* you bind on earth shall be bound in heaven and *<u>whatever</u>* you loose on earth shall be loosed in heaven.*

– Mathew 16:19

I use it on myself and others. I bind my feet to the straight path of Islam. I bind my flesh to the spirit of truth. I bind my will to the will of Allah, my mind to the mind of Jesus, my heart to the smile of God, my tongue to life, my speech to the universe, my faith to the faith of Shadrach, Meshach, and Abednego (Daniel 3:12-25) and my neck to mercy and truth.

Let not mercy and truth forsake thee: bind them about thy neck, write them upon the tablet of thine heart: So shalt thou find favor and good understanding in the sight of God and man.

– Proverbs 3:3-4

I <u>loose</u>, rebuke, destroy and cast out the spirit of error which harbors: impatience—insecurity—independency—laziness—doubt—fear—ignorance—jealousy—idolatry and unbelief. I make sure to loose also the stronghold (door—ego—maingate) that welcomed in the glitched spirit.

P.B.L is an effective God-given power. Afterwards, the universe does its duty. It believes you if you believe "self." Satan knows well the universe as well as the Word of God. That is why the enemy wants you to forget "self." He is the middleman between your speech and the universe. This is his respite. The title of his respite "Prince of the power of the air" (Persia). The universe distinguishes between the Spirit of Truth and the spirit of error, which resides in the sinful flesh of disobedience.

> *Wherein in time past ye walked according to the course of this world, according to the <u>prince of the power of the air</u> [Persia], <u>the spirit</u> that now worketh in the <u>children of disobedience</u>. Among whom also we all had our conversation in times past in the lusts of our flesh, fulfilling the desires of the flesh and of the mind; and were <u>by nature</u> children of wrath.*
>
> *– Ephesians 2:2-3*

Satan watches the devil and capacity of your intent. He then <u>capitalizes</u> on your weakness. Like kryptonite, he is. Seeing where you lack at in all areas that would keep you recoiling (fearfully moving backwards) from the straight path of perfect law, he tricks you only using what he notices the universe dispersing (process of giving) to you. No good thing comes to the devil when you speak into the air for what you hope for because the devil in you simply does not believe it.

Your weakness is brought closer to you to keep you forgetful. If you are a sucker for guns, the universe will bring you before a plethora (bunch) of firearms of diverse (different) kinds, and Satan adds bodies to it before you receive it. This is an example of his capitalization (to make a thing potent). If your weakness is other men of the same sex and you fail to bring the addiction before the Lord God of Abraham, the Faithful, the Merciful, the universe will surely bring the like to you; while before you receive it from the middleman, all sorts of sickness—argument—jealousies and drama are added unto it. If your heart's desire is drugs or money through filth, drugs or dirty money will find you, yet Satan attaches death unto it.

> *But each person is tempted when he is lured and enticed by his own desire. then desire, when it has conceived it gives birth to sin, and sin when it is fully grown brings forth death.*
> — James 1:14-15

"Wherever there is a will (even ill will) you oh universe shall make a way." Remember, the enemy wants only to stir up animosity and hatred among you by mind-altering inventions in order to keep you from prayer and the recollection of who you are and your Maker. Why do we speak into the universe and quickly forget what we command, demand, declare, and decreed? Again:

> *But be ye <u>doers</u> of the word and not hearers only, <u>deceiving yourselves</u>. For if anyone is a <u>hearer</u> of the word and not a <u>doer</u>, he is like a man who looks intently at his <u>natural face</u> [true you] in a mirror. For he looks at <u>himself</u> and goes away and at once [instantly] forgets what he was like. But the one who looks into the <u>perfect law</u> [Islam], the law of liberty, and <u>perseveres</u> [strive] being no <u>hearer who forgets</u> but a doer who acts [remembers to do] will be blessed in his doing.*
> — James 1:22-25

Understand clearly the <u>respite of Satan</u>. He is double minded and so unstable in all his ways. The middleman between you and the universe also has jurisdiction (city limit) between God and man. He has **access to the outer courtyard of heaven**! This is as far as his respite reaches.

> *Now there was a day when the sons of God came to present themselves before the Lord and Satan also came among them to present himself before the Lord.*
>
> – Job 1:6/2:1

And so, "We wrestle against the principalities and spiritual wickedness in high places [Prince of Persia/'power of air']" (see Ephesians 6:12).

You have a few powers left. This next one I call it P.T.A. No, not "pre-trial arrangement," aha, aha. It is the "Power of Touch and Agree." It is a mighty powerful tool, and how awesome it is to encounter another Spirit of Truth to perform it with!

> *Again I say unto you, that if two of you shall <u>agree</u> on Earth as <u>touching anything that they shall ask, it shall be done</u> for them of My Father which is in heaven.*
>
> – Mathew 18:19

Do not abuse this power. Remember, if the other party agrees in spirit, you surely will obtain the desire of your heart.

Ponder on what you are asking for. Think about the possible outcome. Think again of the result it may bring. The request may very well, indeed, bring you before different courses of destruction. Do not perform the P.T.A. with one who harbors the spirit of error. Touch not on any subject with this kind, for though they agree with their lips, inwardly, they disagree.

Identify it by its fruit: impatience—insecurity—independency—laziness—doubt—fear—ignorance—jealousy—idolatry and unbelief. Nevertheless, if any of you lack in discernment, pray for it; for Allah is able to give it to you with ease. Yet if there is one among you with the Spirit of Truth, agree with them for your request, for it brings forth gladness and victory. To find those with the Spirit of Truth, recognize them by their fruit: patience—kindness—peace—love—Joy—gentleness—goodness—faithfulness and self-control.

Here is a secret power you may or may not have heard of. I call it P.C. No, not "Protective Custody," aha, aha. It is immediate "Praise and Clap." Be careful to do this as soon as you receive unwanted news concerning situations and/or circumstances, for as soon as you clap, give praise, and thank God, bad news is immediately <u>reversed upon receiving</u>, for it is confusion to the enemy. Many will fail at these times and instead be carried away with sorrow or rage. Praise and Clap instead, and it shall be reversed.

It causes a <u>shift in the atmosphere</u>. If the news Satan brings you makes you clap, praise, and give thanks to God; he will think he has made a mistake and immediately snatch it back. Nothing the enemy delivers unto you should make you praise and worship God. Nothing! Praise confuses the enemy. Trick him into taking back the bad news concerning circumstances. And this is the virtue (power) we must supplement (installed practice) to our <u>self</u>, <u>putting</u> all these things into practice so that you may be of those left standing when the rest of man falls.

*For this very reason make every effort to supplement your <u>faith</u> with <u>virtue</u>, and virtue with <u>knowledge</u>, and knowledge with <u>self-control</u>, and self-control with <u>patience</u>, and patience with <u>godliness</u>, and godliness with <u>brotherly affection</u> and brotherly affection with **love**. Therefore, brothers be all the more diligent to confirm your calling and <u>election</u>, for <u>if you practice these qualities, you shall never fall.</u>*

– 2 Peter 1:5-7 and 10

After all, didn't Job practice immediate praise upon receiving bad news each time "only one escaped to bring the news"? Do you not know that David, author of psalms, practiced the P.C.? Need I remind you that the P.C. was used by Paul and Silas when the correctional officers fastened their feet in stocks when thrown into the core of the jail (Acts 16:23-26)? Brother, sister, practice these things. You know who you are.

The last power is the purification of the awakening prayer. This is so powerful that God said, "<u>Purify</u> and <u>prostrate</u> thyself to perform the prayers when you <u>awake</u> and you can be <u>for</u> <u>certain</u> I will be standing <u>on your right, beside you</u>." When you awake, the first prayer is a special kind, and it is to be purified. <u>God instructs you</u>; when you arise, you <u>must</u> wash your hands and your arms up to your elbows. Wash your face. Wipe your head and wash your feet up to the ankle (I take it upon myself to go the extra mile by brushing my teeth first and showering to purify the whole body).

This purification creates an invisible barrier over the prayer that spiritual wickedness in high places cannot handle. The enemy is given respite over the air and often attempts to interfere with your prayer as it rises. The purified prayers are immediately heard and are prayers that the enemy is enraged against and so willing to war with angels over. The purified prayers do not have to be placed in containers where incense must be added or offered alongside it before it is presented to God by prayer collecting angels (Revelation 8:3). The purified prostration is spiritually fierce.

> *...then the angel said to me "Fear not, Daniel: for from the first day, you <u>prostrated</u> yourself and became humble before Allah, your <u>prayer was heard</u> and I am come because of your prayer. The prince of the kingdom of Persia [prince of the power of the air] withstood me 21 days but Michael [the archangel] one of the chief princes came*

to help me, for I was left there with the <u>Kings of Persia</u> [Satan and the 665].

– Daniel 10:12-13

And these are your gifts, your authority, your name, your identity, your creation, your lineage, and practices.

*Do not neglect *the gift* you have which was <u>given you by prophecy</u> when the <u>*council of elders laid their hands on you</u>* Practice these <u>things, immerse</u> (drown) <u>yourself in them</u> so that all may see your progress. Keep a close watch on yourself and *the teaching*. <u>Persist in this</u> for <u>by doing so you save yourself and your hearers</u>.*

– 1 Timothy 4:14-16

You are a chosen black nation of God. He stretched out the heavens and laid the foundations of the Earth in six days. You are a people—set apart—for His own possession (1 Peter 2:9).

And ye shall be holy unto me: for I am holy, I, the Lord has severed you from other people, that ye should be mine.

– Leviticus 20:26

But what about other races?

10

Jesus, the Mystery of God

And this, this is the divine conspiracy! The very symbol of God's (agape) love and grace. Allah, the Gracious, the Merciful: There is no God but He who knew afore time, <u>in the</u> <u>beginning</u> that not only the offspring of Abraham should enjoy salvation; but through a special kind of partial sacrifice never before seen and unheard of shall <u>all manner of people *share*</u> in the glory and salvation of the chosen "tents of Judah."

> *And the Lord will give salvation to the <u>tents of Judah *first*</u> that <u>the glory</u> of the <u>house of David</u> and the glory of the inhabitants of Jerusalem *may not surpass that of Judah*.*
>
> *– Zechariah 12:7*

Jesus and the purpose of becoming is the mystery of God. Jesus, the Christ, the Messiah, the Mahdi (in your original language) means "God in the Person" (flesh). He was a <u>mirror</u> of the Lord God Almighty.

> *He [Jesus] is the radiance of the glory of God and <u>exact</u> <u>imprint</u> of <u>His nature</u>...*
>
> *– Hebrews 1:3*

He was fully trained and complete in oneness with Yahweh yet did not count himself equal with God.

> *…who though he was in the form of God, did not count equality with God…*
> — Philippians 2:6

> *A disciple is not above his teacher but <u>everyone</u> when he is <u>fully trained</u> will be <u>like</u> his teacher.*
> — Luke 6:40

He was not at all begotten in a sexual sense. This is an insult to God. Jesus was *__adopted__* by God when He was <u>fully trained</u> on *the day* John baptized Him; thus, making Him Messenger of messengers, Son of sons, and King of kings.

> *For unto which of the angels said He at any time, Thou art my <u>Son</u>, *__this day__* <u>have I begotten thee</u>? And again, I will be to him a Father and he shall be to me a Son?*
> — Hebrews 1:5

> *I will declare the decree: the Lord hath said unto me, Thou art my Son; *__this day__* <u>have I begotten thee.</u>*
> — Psalm 2:7

And **this day** was the moment of adoption where Jesus inherited the name "Son of God." He was the "Son of Man" and respected the title, calling Himself at all times "<u>Son of Man</u>," His identity.

> *But that you may know that the <u>Son of Man</u> has authority on earth to forgive sins…*
> — Matthew 9:6

Jesus said:

The days are coming when you will desire to see one of the days of the <u>Son of Man</u> and you will not see it.

– Luke 17:22

For as the lightning cometh out of <u>the east</u>, and shineth even unto <u>the west</u>; so shall also the coming of the <u>Son of Man</u> be.

– Matthew 24: 27

Just as it was in the days of Noah, so will it be in the days of the <u>Son of Man</u>.

– Luke 17:26

Truly, truly I say unto you, you will see heaven opened up and the angels of God ascending (going up) and descending (going down) on the <u>Son of Man</u>.

–John 1:51

He was greater than the prophets, higher than the angels and Messenger of messengers, just as Muhammad (peace be upon him) was his like. And the name "Son of God" is through adoption.

*Being made so much better than the angels, as he hath **<u>by inheritance</u>** obtained a <u>more excellent</u> name [Son of God] than they.*

– Hebrews 1:4

For Jesus has been counted <u>more worthy of glory</u> than Moses.

– Hebrews 3:3

Moses was the only human in his uniqueness to <u>see</u> <u>God</u> face to face (Numbers 12:7-8, Exodus 33:11).

> *[Jesus] far <u>above all rule</u> and <u>authority</u> and <u>power</u> and <u>dominion</u> and <u>above</u> <u>every name</u> that is named, not only in this age but also in the one to come.*
>
> – Ephesians 1:21

And this was His rank. He came to suffer to the point of death, and this was <u>the work</u>. That all mankind may partake (share) in the salvation of the <u>children of Israel</u>, which are a separate people.

> *Remember that you [all others] were at that time separated from Christ, alienated [singled out] from the <u>common wealth of Israel</u> and <u>strangers</u> to the <u>covenants of promise</u>, having no hope and <u>without God</u> in the world.*
>
> – Ephesians 2:12

> *What I mean is that each one of you says "I am of Paul" or "I follow Apollos" or "I follow Cephas" or "I follow Christ."*
>
> – 1 Corinthians 1:12

We all serve the same God. There is only one God, one faith, and Jesus serves only Him. Under God comes Jesus, their Mediator, their Lord, and Savior.

Through Jesus, the hostility between a people is abolished (no more).

> *For through him (Jesus) we <u>both</u> have <u>access</u> in <u>one spirit</u> to the Father. So then you are <u>no</u> <u>longer strangers and aliens</u> but you are <u>fellow citizens</u> <u>*with the saints*</u> and members of the household of God.*
>
> – Ephesians 2:18-19

And to him (Jesus) was given dominion and glory and a <u>kingdom</u> that <u>all people, nations</u>, and <u>languages</u> should serve him...”

– Daniel 7:14

Glory to God for such grace.

*Giving thanks to the father who has <u>qualified you</u> (all others) to <u>*share*</u> in the inheritance of <u>the saints</u> (chosen black nation) in light.*

– 1 Colossians 1:12

This mystery is that the gentiles are fellow hairs, members of the same body and partakers of the promise in Christ Jesus through the gospel.

– Ephesians 3:6

Jesus suffered to the point of death for six hours. From the third hour to the ninth hour, he did <u>the work</u>. He was not killed but was told by our Father: <u>“Come up here!”</u> By His own power Jesus <u>gave up his spirit *before time*</u>. And He appeared dead as though He was killed, yet it was only by the Spirit absent from the body, for Jesus “died” too soon.

But when they came to Jesus <u>and saw that he was already dead</u>, they did not break his legs.

– John 19:33

He did not die. Understand this: Our brother Jesus gave up his Spirit by His <u>say so</u>.

No man taketh from me, but I lay it down of myself. I have power to lay it down and I have power to take it again. This commandment I have received of my Father.

– John 10:18

Shocking to you, but true to us. For this reason, the bystanders who witnessed the spectacle were shocked also.

> *Then Jesus calling out with a loud voice, said, "Father into your hands I commit my spirit!" And <u>having said this</u> he breathed his last. Now when the centurion [chief watchguard] saw what had taken place [the fashion in which His Spirit escaped] he praised God saying, "Certainly this man was innocent!" And all the crowds that was assembled for this spectacle when they saw what had taken place [how his Spirit yielded to his say so] returned home beating their breasts.*
>
> – Luke 23:46-48

> *And Jesus cried out with a loud voice and yielded up his spirit.*
>
> – Mathew 27:50

Jesus, at that moment, was reunited with God for three-and-a-half human days. In crucifixion, the normalcy of human decomposition is a gruesome grievance of 72 hours, and towards the end of it, the centurion was to confirm death by the breaking of one's bones to speed the process of death by neglect. In the case of Jesus, it was written as scripture: "None of his bones will be broken." By His own power, Jesus left His own body before the point of death for <u>the work</u> He came to accomplish was finished through suffering and heartbrokenness.

The Gospel of Mark best describes this doing:

> *And when the centurion who stood facing him (Jesus) <u>*saw that in this way*</u> he breathed his last, he said "truly this man was the Son of God."*
>
> – Mark 15:39

Jesus ascended before they could pierce his side (19:34) for God did not will for His Son to feel that type of pain.

*Pilate [king-judge] <u>was surprised to hear</u> <u>that he</u> [Jesus] should have
<u>already</u> <u>died</u>. And when he [Pilate] learned from the centurion that
he [Jesus] was dead, he [Pilate] granted the corpse [a body lacking
components of life] to Joseph.*

– Mark 15:44-45

So you see, he did not die but was told "Come up here!"

(Revelation 11:12).

What a conspiracy from the beginning of time. From the beginning, Jesus was and is the Word and "Light"; the true light from the beginning of Earth's formation. Though He was the first light from which God said, "Let there be light," and behold, Jesus was born by the breath of God's say so; He too was volunteered (Revelation 5:5-9) to be reborn and placed in his mother's stomach without the need to be planted in a human, for Jesus was not made by a mixture of a liquid sperm drop. Just like Adam, He emerged into formation by the word of God! Amen.

And this is the mystery.

*Making known to us the mystery of his will, according to his purpose
which he set forth in Christ Jesus <u>as a plan for the fullness of time</u>, to
<u>unite all</u> things in heaven and earth in him.*

– Ephesians 1:9-10

*He predestined us [all others] for <u>adoption</u> as sons through <u>Jesus
Christ</u>, according to his will and purpose.*

– Ephesians 1:5

*...the mystery hidden for ages and generations but now revealed to
<u>his saints</u>. To them [the chosen] God chose to make known how great*

And so, Jesus existed in the realm of what is unseen before coming into
existence unto the world which is the realm that is visible.

11

Picture Him

Our brother Jesus, our Helper, a 5'8 black man of <u>Nazareth</u>, a dread head like Samson.

...but you shall conceive and bear a son. Therefore, be careful and drink no wine and eat nothing unclean, for behold, ye shall conceive and bare a son. <u>No razor</u> shall come upon his head, for the child shall be a <u>Nazarite</u> to God from the womb...

– Judges 13:3-5

Like wool were the hairs on his head (Revelation 1:14-16, Daniel 7:9). Be not fooled. Jesus, like Moses and Abraham, was <u>monotheist</u> (Muslim), for this is not a religion you choose; it is who you are. Man's pure nature which God gave you, saying, "Today, I have perfected it for you. I give you Islam as your religion. It is My straight path in which ye are to walk and follow."

And you are of the AB-original descendants; Those who distorted the Book and titled it "Holy" to further keep you lost, renamed you. Your original language is Arabic, which was stripped from your ancestors during the 400 years of slavery. Today, we do not speak our original language. We speak English; the language of our forefathers' slave owner. Your race is not African American; it is Hebrew Israelite. You are offspring of the Hebrew slaves of Egypt. You are Islam; the nature made by Allah in which He has created men. Don't you know that you are gods? You are gods!

12

No Good Job at Distortion, Part 1

The distorters did no good job at distorting all the word of God. They left "You are gods" in a few places. And removing every "black" word (which is still in every King James version Bible of 1611) and replacing it with "dark" to further keep you forgetful. For example, Song of Solomon 1:5-6:

I am very dark, but lovely…Do not gaze at me because I am dark…

And they added verses like Exodus 21:20-21:

When a man strikes [hits] his slave, male or female with a rod and the slave dies under his hand, he shall be avenged but if the slave survives a day or two, he is not to be avenged, for the slave is his money.

Not so: These words are not spoken from the Lord your God. And many more.

Adding more knowledge to you concerning the first of the pages in the Bible placed by the Gideons 2013, you shall locate the *Copyright Information* page. Follow along with me starting halfway mark the fourth line through the seventh line:

...up to and inclusive of [1000] verses without express written permission of the publisher, provided that the verses quoted <u>do not</u> amount to a complete Book of the Bible nor do the verses quoted account for <u>50% or more</u> of the total text of <u>the work</u> in which they are quoted.

(Stripping off meaning also.)

Listen, every promise of God belongs to you. You know who you are. You only become gods when you are "woke" [spiritually aware] and can identify self.

So, what is your name, my brother? What is your name, sister? It is a beautiful name, and there is none like it. Exercise your powers, and walk like your Maker created you and you shall be more than conquerors. As for those of you who are not the chosen generation, worry not, for you have been counted in through <u>our Helper</u> and <u>Brother</u> Jesus, your Lord God and Savior.

He helps the offspring of Abraham.

– Hebrew 2:16

*For you separated *them* from among <u>all the peoples</u> of the earth to be Your heritage..."*

– 1 Kings 8:53

Praise the Lamb of God, your God Jesus, <u>our Brother</u>.

Therefore he had to be made like his brothers in every respect...

– Hebrews 2:17

We obey God and His Messenger. They never disagree. We serve only God, for it is a direct order to the chosen. There is only One and none besides God.

He often repeats: "I alone am the Lord God," and "Before the beginning, by myself, I Am," and "Never shall you serve any God but me."

Thus says the Lord, the King of Israel and his (Israel's) Redeemer, the Lord of hosts: "I am the first and the last; besides me there is no God. Who is like me? Let him proclaim it. Let him declare and set it before me, since I appointed an ancient people. Let them declare what is to come, and what will happen. Fear not nor be afraid; have I not told you from old and declared it? And you are my witnesses! Is there a God besides me? there is no Rock; I know not any."

– Isaiah 44:6-8

So, call on Allah by whatever title you call on Him; He has the best of names. "He is Allah besides Whom there is no God: The Knower of the unseen and the seen; He is the Beneficent, the Merciful. He is Allah besides Whom there is no God; the King, the Holy, the Author of Peace, the Granter of Security, Guardian over all, the Mighty, the Supreme, the Possessor of greatness. Glory be to Allah from that which they set up (with Him)! He is Allah; the Creator, the Maker, the Fashioner: His are the most beautiful names. Whatever is in the heavens and the earth declare His glory; and He is the Mighty, the Wise" {59:22-24}. Know for certain that there is no God but Allah (all 99 names of God), and when one calls out to Allah, he calls upon the Lord God in 99 ways.

God created 12 major and 12 minor scientists who have power to prophesy up to 5,000 years, and in them, there is no flaw and nothing false. The elders obey instruction and fall to worship Him, saying, "Thou art worthy, O Lord, to receive glory and honour and power: for Thou hast created all things, and for thy pleasure they are and were created." This happens every time the four beastly creatures say, "Holy,

Holy, Holy, Lord God Almighty, which was and is, and is to come!" If the distorters had not tainted the Book, you would have found an account of these things in the last book of the Book in 1:75-82. Instead, it is in 4:4-11.

You who have our Brother Jesus as your Lord and Savior, we welcome you with immense joy. We remember Paul's foolish bragging and boasting, saying, as if he were you now being able to say, **"Are they Hebrew? So am I. Are they Israelites? So am I. Are they offspring of Abraham? So am I"** (2 Corinthians 11:22). For you are children of light, and we saints are children of God. Our Brother Jesus told us, "… I will tell of your name to my brothers…I will put my trust in him [the trust of Jesus will be inside you] Behold, I and the *<u>children God has given me</u>*" (Hebrews 2:12-13), thereby making you included. According to Romans 1:6 and 14: "Including you who are called to *<u>belong</u>* to Jesus Christ" … "I [Paul] am under obligation [to proclaim the gospel of Jesus] both **to the Greeks** and **to barbarians**."

13

Assigning Your Petition to Whom It May Concern

Finally, the Lord God, the Beneficent, the Merciful, hears every cry. Not even a whisper of an idea goes unnoticed. Thus says the Lord, "Though you assign to thy petition the signature of him who I declared my Son by my permission gave I unto him power to rule over the lost and not found; Ye who finds himself shall address it (at the ending of prayer) by the God of truth."

> *So that he who blesses himself in the land shall bless himself <u>by the God of truth</u>, and he who takes an oath in the land shall swear <u>by the God of truth</u>; because the former troubles are forgotten and hidden from my eyes.*
>
> – Isaiah 65:16

Yes, God. Amen

Although there is no wrong in praying in the name of prophets and in the name of Jesus, which carries a tremendous mighty weight of glory, it is wise much to pray in the Spirit **by the God of Truth,** which holds an exceeding and far more eternal weight of glory (2 Corinthians 4:17). For you know the effectual fervent prayer of the righteous ones has great power (James 5:16).

Let us therefore Strive to enter that rest, so that no one may fall by
the same sort of disobedience.

– Hebrews 4:11

"And those who strive hard for Us, We shall certainly guide them in Our ways. And Allah is surely with the doers of good" {29:69}.

"And whoso desires the Hereafter and strives for it as he ought to strive and he is a believer—those are they whose striving is amply rewarded" {17:19}.

Warners you are; all of you. Warn them all, I say. By doing so in just this, you may show thyself approved through knowledge and belief.

PEACE BE UNTO YOU
in your original tongue.
A S S A L A M U A L A I K U M

14

No Good Job at Distortion, Part 2

Since your scales have fallen, I am more than confident in your sight to solve a thing. There was one whom his history and true identity were <u>removed</u> from the Book. Who was he? (Revelation 11:3-13 and Zechariah 4:3-13)

9 798888 729285 4